Original title:
Wrapped in Christmas Magic

Copyright © 2024 Creative Arts Management OÜ
All rights reserved.

Author: Micah Sterling
ISBN HARDBACK: 978-9916-94-066-2
ISBN PAPERBACK: 978-9916-94-067-9

Letters to Santa Under the Stars

The paper's crumpled, the ink's a mess,
My dog ate my list, I must confess.
I ask for a bike, but write 'can of beans',
Santa's confused, but I'm still keen.

The stars are bright, I'll leave him snacks,
Some chips and dip, and a box of tacks.
I hope he laughs when he reads my note,
Then zooms by in his magical coat.

Candles Flicker in Winter's Embrace

The candles flicker, the shadows dance,
While Uncle Bob spills his eggnog by chance.
The cat's in the tree, oh what a sight,
He swears he's a reindeer, ready for flight.

Grandma's baking cookies, oh what a smell,
She burns the batch, but we'll never tell.
With frosting on faces and laughs all around,
In this cozy chaos, joy can be found.

A Hearth Full of Hope

The fire crackles, it's warm and bright,
Grandpa's snoring, it's quite a sight.
The stockings are hung, but Daddy tripped,
Now they're all on the floor, fully stripped!

A mug of cocoa, a marshmallow float,
A reindeer puppet, a funny coat.
With giggles and grins, we share the cheer,
This silly chaos brings us near.

A Spectrum of Holiday Melodies

The carolers sing off key once more,
Barking dogs join in, it's a festive score.
While Aunt Sue's dancing in the wrong pair of shoes,
We laugh so hard, we've forgotten the blues.

The tunes are silly, yet filled with glee,
While Cousin Joe sings like a bumblebee.
It's a concert of joy, a cacophony bliss,
In this holiday jam, we can't help but miss.

Lyrics of Joy in the Crisp Air

Snowflakes dance, like little sprites,
It's time for snowball fights!
With hot cocoa spilling in my cup,
I sip and slip, whoops, down I plop!

Jingle bells ring, the dog starts to bark,
Chasing candy canes out in the dark!
Whiskers twitch and wagging tails,
Santa's nine reindeer leave goofy trails!

Comets of Laughter in Flurries

Elves on the shelf, plotting their schemes,
To sneak cookies while we steal dreams!
Christmas lights twinkle, causing a blight,
I trip on the rug, oh what a sight!

Reindeer games around the tree,
Pine needles prank my poor old knee!
Wrappers flying in a frenzied spin,
Why did I think this was a win?

A Journey through a Festive Dreamscape

Gingerbread houses start to shake,
I swear they move for heaven's sake!
Cookies crunch beneath my heel,
I hope those were not meant for a meal!

Tinsel tangled in my hair,
Oh dear, what a festive scare!
Santa's lap—a bumpy ride,
What's this? More milk? I confide!

Glowing Hearts and Misty Dreams

Mittens mismatched, I roam through snow,
Falling face-first, my face aglow!
Carols warble from off-key friends,
Yet laughter and joy never shall end!

Stockings hung but maybe too far,
The cat thinks they're his personal car!
In this cheerful, snowy delight,
Who knew chaos could be so bright?

Secrets Etched in the Snow

Snowflakes dance, a cheeky flurry,
Sledding kids in a wild hurry.
Frosty noses, laughter bright,
Snowball fights that last till night.

Carrots lost, on snowmen's heads,
Sticks for arms, misplaced in beds.
Secret whispers, bundled tight,
Hot cocoa warms the chilly bite.

The Beauty of a Season's Gift.

Packages wrapped with bows that tease,
Dogs unroll them with such ease.
Tinsel tangled, a festive mess,
Cats pretend they couldn't care less.

Jingle bells play a pranky tune,
While cookies vanish too soon.
Grandma's sweater, too bright a sight,
Makes you giggle, what a delight!

Winter's Enchantment

Icicles hang like teeth of frost,
But hot pies warm the party lost.
Pine tree smells like whispering cheer,
As neighbors fight for whose lights are sheer.

Snowmen with smiles so wide and round,
Busy penguins shuffle all around.
Christmas tunes and silly glee,
Echo in halls, 'Oh look! It's me!'

The Glimmer of Holiday Dreams

Chasing after a rogue reindeer,
Who's stealing cookies, what a fear!
Wrapped presents hold surprises tight,
But all you see is colorful fright.

Stockings hang, overstuffed and grand,
With odd-shaped goodies, all unplanned.
Twinkling lights in a grand array,
Dance like fireflies in dismay.

A Season's Caress

Snowflakes tumble, flinging wide,
Socks on reindeer, laugh beside.
Gifts stacked high, the cat's in trance,
Cousins dance in awkward pants.

Mistletoe hangs, oops! shoe's caught,
Grandpa's snoring, oh, what a thought!
Cookies vanish, crumbs all around,
Elves on break, but still astound.

Whispering Pines and Holiday Cheer

Pine-scented air, a squirrel's delight,
Giggling kids in woolly tights.
Lights like disco balls on trees,
A dance party with buzz and sleaze.

Hot cocoa spills, marshmallows fly,
Uncle Joe's jokes always do pry.
Snowmen wobble, noses askew,
Penguins in sweaters—who knew?

Trails of Sugar and Spice

Gingerbread houses, oh what a mess,
Frosting fights lead to pure excess.
Candy canes starting to melt,
Chasing the dog who just won't be dealt.

Bells jingle, but wait, what's that?
The partridge is stuck; poor bird's flat!
Plates piled high with treats galore,
Molasses sneezes, laughter's in store.

The Joys of Evergreen Embrace

Twinkling lights wrapped round the cat,
Santa's sleigh is now a hat.
Frosty cups froth over frosty cheer,
Ticklish toes, come dance from here!

Laughter bubbles, jokes so wrong,
A tree that's leaning, can't be long.
Surprises hidden in every bite,
New Year's diet? Not tonight!

Snowflakes Dancing on the Breeze

Snowflakes tumble, oh what a sight,
Making snowmen, pure delight.
The dog's confused, he leaps and bounds,
Chasing those flakes, lost in the sounds.

Kids giggle, slipping on their shoes,
Under the trees, they dodge and cruise.
Each snowball flies, a soft hit here,
Oh, what a winter! Let's all cheer!

A Symphony of Joyful Chimes

Bells ring out from every door,
Tap-dancing Santa, hear the roar!
Elves in a jam, they're stuck in glue,
Trying to fix a sleigh that flew.

Cookies baked with a dash of fun,
Chef's hat askew, it's a wild run!
Sprinkle fights, flour in the air,
Whiskers twitching, oh the flair!

Candles Glow in Silent Reverie

Candles flicker, shadows play,
Oops! That one's gone, what a display!
Cats chase the lights, a furry mess,
As kids hide sweets, oh what finesse!

Honey-glazed hams, they spark delight,
But grandpa snores, what a funny sight!
Laughter bubbles, a feast so grand,
Jokes fly around like a merry band!

Sparkling Eyes and Warm Hearts

Sparkling eyes, mischief in stare,
Presents are wrapped with a twist of flair.
The dog found a shoe, oh what a fright,
Nibbling gifts deep into the night.

Wrapping paper, a dance on the floor,
Tangled up tightly, we stumble and roar.
Each gift giggles, they're eager to please,
Opening moments, a flurry of tease!

Harmonies of Hope in the Chill

Snowflakes dance with glee,
Singing tunes of pure delight.
Hot cocoa spills on my knee,
As I laugh at my own plight.

Frosty noses poke and tease,
Jingle bells ring loud and bright.
Carrots lost in winter's breeze,
Sledding down till late at night.

The Art of Giving and Warm Embrace

Gift wrap fights with unseen hands,
Tangled bows that mock my aim.
Each unwrapped joy expands,
And laughter is the sweetest game.

Cookies made with extra cheer,
Flour's cloud creates a scene.
Santa's belly shakes with beer,
While kids yell out, 'We're the dream team!'

A Canvas of Sparkling Memories

Twinkling lights on every tree,
A cat climbs high, oh what a sight!
Fallen ornaments set me free,
As they shimmer in the night.

Neighbors eye each other's kits,
Whose lawn's the brightest—what a feat!
Tinsel fights turn into skits,
With laughter echoing down the street.

Hearts Entwined by Winter's Spell

Socks are tossed across the floor,
And I trip over holiday cheer.
Wobbling kids rush to the door,
All the while, I sip my beer.

Candles flicker, shadows play,
A roast burns as the night unfolds.
Granny's jokes—oh, what a day!
Each punchline makes this madness gold.

Frost-Kissed Wishes on the Wind

Snowflakes dance like silly geese,
On cheerful rooftops, joy won't cease.
Reindeer giggle, slipping much too fast,
Chasing elves who're flying past!

Cookies crumble, frosting flies,
Giggling kids share funny sighs.
Hot cocoa spills, a marshmallow fight,
In this winter wonder, all feels right!

Echoes of Laughter Through the Pines

Pine trees sway, they seem to grin,
While squirrels plot mischief from within.
Snowmen wobble in their hats so tall,
As hats fly off with a wintry squall!

Laughter bounces through the frosty air,
Santa trips on gifts without a care.
The stars above twinkle with delight,
As jolly souls dance through the night!

Secrets Beneath the Mistletoe

Underneath that ball of green,
Kisses stolen, oh what a scene!
Grandma's stories, silly and bold,
Make the lit-up room feel like gold.

The cat hides, plotting her sweet attack,
While cousins sneak in for a snack.
As laughter rings from room to room,
Mistletoe's magic dispels all gloom!

Radiance in the Quiet of Night

Twinkling lights, oh what a sight,
Whispers of joy dance in the night.
The moon winks down with a knowing laugh,
As the snowmen take a silly bath!

Jingle bells echo, a mischievous tune,
With giggles bubbling like a festoon.
While dreams take flight on this starry air,
Christmas cheer spreads everywhere!

Whispers of Winter's Embrace

Snowflakes giggle as they fall,
Dancing down like a feathered ball.
Hot cocoa spills, a chocolate stream,
As marshmallows dive in like they dream.

Jingle bells start to play a tune,
The cat's in the tree, wrapped like a boon.
With twinkling lights that flicker and sigh,
That weird snowman, it blinks an eye.

Cookies vanish, the plate is bare,
Santa's elves brought their wild affair.
A sled rides high on a hill of ice,
Oh look! It's a pup, oh so precise!

Frosty breath and laughter loud,
In this winter wonderland, we're proud.
With each silly slip and a joyful shout,
We make merry, no room for doubt.

Enchanted Nights Beneath the Stars

Under twinkling skies so bright,
We chase the snowflakes, what a sight!
A snowman wears a jaunty hat,
While nearby, there sits a sneaky cat.

Hot cider spills, a warm delight,
We sing off-key, a comical sight.
Tangled lights, what a crazy mess,
Just one more try, I must confess.

The moon grins big, it's quite the tease,
As snowmen dance, they bend their knees.
Reindeer prance with a wink and grin,
In this silly frolic, we all begin.

With laughter echoing through the night,
Each moment feels so very right.
Comrades in jests, not a care in sight,
Beneath the stars, we share delight.

Tinsel Dreams and Frosty Breath

Tinsel shines like a disco ball,
Hanging low, ready to enthrall.
Our tree's so bright it lights the room,
A cat climbs high, oh what a zoom!

Frosty breath turns into clouds,
We giggle and jump, we're so proud.
Eggnog spilled on grandma's shoes,
"Oh dear!" she yelps, while we all snooze.

Carols sung with off-tune glee,
Who knew we'd sound like a buzzing bee?
Rudolph sneezes, it's quite the scene,
A laugh erupts, oh, what a meme!

With every bell and every cheer,
We make new jokes year after year.
Wrapping up in comical flair,
Creating memories beyond compare.

The Gift of Radiant Light

Beneath the tree, a pile of glee,
Each present wrapped, oh can't you see!
A sweater's knitted, a llama's face,
A gift that's sure to win the race!

Lights are tangled, it's a sight,
Dad shakes his head in sheer delight.
"What's this?" he says, a mysterious box,
"Oh dear," exclaims mom, "it's filled with socks!"

The dog steals a cupcake from the plate,
As children giggle, they can't wait.
A game of hide and seek starts quick,
While grandma's snoring, oh so thick.

In the mix of mischief and cheer,
We spread the warmth, year after year.
Joy is wrapped in laughter tight,
Together, we shine, a dazzling light.

Starlit Wishes on a Frosty Night

Tinsel hangs like wild hair,
While snowflakes dance without a care.
Cookies placed without a thought,
Santa might just eat the lot!

Gifts stacked high and all askew,
Whispers carry tales anew.
Reindeer prance on rooftops bright,
Who knew they'd cause such a fright?

Eggnog spills on the cat's new bed,
While tree limbs wobble—oh, the dread!
Laughter echoes through the air,
As squirrels plot their holiday dare.

Frosted windows hide our cheer,
While neighbors complain a bit too near.
Jingle bells ring some chaos deep,
Who knew such joy made us lose sleep?

A Gentle Embrace of Memories

Family photos in disarray,
Grandma's fruitcake, oh what a play!
Laughter bubbles like hot cocoa,
While we pretend to be like pros.

Ornaments tossed, some land on the floor,
Each a story we can't ignore.
Mismatched socks tell their own tale,
While mistletoe finds its own trail.

Pine needles dance beneath our feet,
As we compete for the best seat.
Giggles echo through the air,
When someone's trying to find their chair.

Stories shared, some tall and wide,
With half the truth and lots of pride.
As laughter fills every room,
We wonder how much space for gloom?

Dreamscapes Sprinkled with Snow

Fluffy clouds in the night sky,
With each big snowflake, a soft sigh.
Kids with sleds speeding downhill,
While adults pretend they feel just ill.

Hot cocoa spills and smiles arise,
As marshmallows fly like tiny spies.
The snowman wobbles, then tips over,
Who knew frostbite could bring such fervor?

Winter's chill makes noses red,
As playful snowballs zoom overhead.
Frosty cheeks with grins so wide,
No one thought they'd take that ride!

As stars twinkle and sparkle bright,
We dance around till the first light.
With joy and laughter held so dear,
Who knew cold could warm our cheer?

The Glow of Friendship and Light

Balloons float and lights twinkle,
Matching socks? Just a crinkle!
Friends gather, tinsel in their hair,
Unruly chaos, laughter in the air.

Laughter shared over half-eaten pies,
As we ignore the cookie lies.
Gifts exchanged, surprise or not,
"Did you really get me this whole lot?"

Party hats perched at odd angles,
As we dodge jokes like silly dangles.
Music blares, feet move in time,
Who knew friendship could feel like a rhyme?

With every sip of punch we cheer,
Our silly tales banish all fear.
Together under the sparkling lights,
We'll laugh and dance through magical nights!

A Tapestry of Twinkling Lights

In the glow of lights, so bright,
Santas juggling in mid-flight.
Elves on ladders, tangled cheer,
Hilarity wraps the atmosphere.

Gingerbread men start to dance,
Spinning round, they seize their chance.
With frosting hats that gleam and shine,
They trip on candy, fall in line.

Sparkles twinkle in the night,
Reindeer flying by in flight.
Snowflakes giggle, land with glee,
Like children playing hide and see.

So let's toast with cocoa cups,
To all the joy that fills us up.
We'll laugh and share this festive time,
In a world that jingles like a rhyme.

Embraced by Frosted Whispers

Frosted windows, a sight to see,
Snowmen waving cheerfully.
One lost a hat, oh what a sight,
As he honks a horn with all his might.

Sipping cocoa, I spill some too,
On my sweater—what can I do?
Elf on a shelf with a wink and grin,
Eyes moving fast, let the games begin.

Tinsel tangled in my hair,
Sprinkled glitter everywhere.
When the carols start to play,
The cat joins in, steals the sleigh!

Laughter echoes through the night,
Neighbors shouting, "What a sight!"
With mistletoe hanging, hearts aglow,
We savor moments, bask in the show.

The Spirit of Yuletide Wonders

Stockings hung with silly toys,
Filled with goodies, oh what joys!
A partridge in a box of cheer,
Singing loud for all to hear.

The tree's so tall, it sways and bends,
As pets climb up instead of friends.
Ornaments tumble, yet we just laugh,
Finding peace in our silly path.

Cards with photos that don't align,
Grandma's eyes, yet only half a mime.
We'll gather 'round, tell tales anew,
Of goofy facts none ever knew.

So hear the jingle, dance and sing,
Let all our hearts just take to wing.
This time of year, with humor bright,
We spark the joy, ignite the night.

Allure of the Glistening Eve

Underneath a sky of stars,
Santa's lost his way, oh dear!
The reindeer nibble on cookie jars,
While elves are playing truth or cheer.

With snowy boots, we make a mess,
Sledding down, we do our best.
Hot chocolate spills, laughter loud,
No one's mean, we're all just proud.

Lights all flicker like a dance,
As we prance around in our snow pants.
A snowball flies, oh what a hit!
Laughter erupts; we never quit.

So let's embrace this happy night,
With all our friends, holding tight.
We'll sip the joys, and let love please,
In our quirkiness, we find our ease.

Hearthside Serenade

The cat's on the mantle, eyeing the stew,
A dance of delight in a fuzzy old shoe.
Uncle Joe's snoring, a real lullaby,
While Aunt May's trying to bake, oh my!

Bright lights are twinkling like stars gone mad,
The dog's in a sweater, oh isn't he sad?
Gifts piled high, yet he snatched one, oh dear,
That squeaky toy causing a whirlwind of cheer!

Hot cocoa spills in a playful big splash,
"Did I do that?" as the marshmallows clash.
Little Timmy's giggles, a ringing delight,
Making memories on this jolly, bright night.

With jokes and laughter that fill up the air,
All bundled together, we've not a care.
As we dance 'round the fire, a whimsical tease,
This hearthside serenade brings us to our knees.

Frosty Kisses and Candlelight Wishes

Snow's tumbling down in a flurry of fun,
While we sip on our cocoa and plot to outrun.
A snowman with carrots, oh, what a silly sight,
With a hat that's too big for his head, what a plight!

Fingers all chilly, we puff out our breath,
Building snow forts like we conquer our heft.
But wait! Here comes Fido, he dives in the mix,
Taking down snowmen!

Oh, what a fix!

Candles are glowing, and candles are sway,
As Grandma recounts her wild youthful play.
But Uncle Bob whispers, "I see what you're missing!"
A juicy mystery that leaves us all guessing!

Frosty kisses linger, and laughter takes flight,
With holiday wishes that sparkle so bright.
So raise up your cup, may the giggles stay near,
In this winter wonderland, filled with good cheer!

Echoes of Joyful Laughter

Chasing the kids as they dash down the lane,
A pie in the face? Oh, isn't it plain?
Grandpa is hiding, a wild prankster's art,
With a turkey costume, he plays the part!

The ornaments jingle, a tune oh so spry,
As Dad turns around, and oh my, oh my!
A dance with the vacuum? How strange, but fun,
It's a party at home, we've only begun.

The tinsel is shiny, but so is Aunt Sue,
"Don't eat that!" she warns, "That's meant for the view!"
Laughter erupts like confetti in glee,
While we contemplate who'll climb up the tree.

Echoes of laughter fill every room,
With the scent of sweet cookies that brightly bloom.
We gather together, in joy we all bask,
In this festive mischief, we need no more tasks!

Under the Starry Canopy

Beneath a bright sky, we gather outside,
With twinkling lights on a sled that won't glide.
"Is that the star?" points little Lou,
As we giggle and laugh at the squirrels so few.

Fingers all tangled in garland and cheer,
A snowball to catch? Wait, not in the ear!
Pine needles prick at our legs like a joke,
While Grandma says, "Be careful with that smoke!"

Hot cookies come out, fresh from the box,
A riot of sprinkles, chocolate, and clocks.
We toast with our cups filled with fizzy delight,
At this magical gathering, all's merry and bright.

Under the stars, with a chorus of cheer,
We find such a joy that we hold ever dear.
From laughter to giggles, we're lost in this flight,
Under the starry canopy, everything feels right.

The Melody of Twinkling Lights

Singing bulbs on strings so bright,
Dance around in festive delight.
Elves on stilts, a comical sight,
As snowflakes fall in soft twilight.

A cat in a hat, oh what a scene,
Chasing shadows, it's quite routine.
Tinsel adorns a tree far and wide,
While puppies chew on the lights with pride.

The mistletoe hangs, no place to hide,
As Uncle Joe winks, full of pride.
A dance-off begins, it's pure holiday fun,
With moves so silly, it can't be outdone.

So let laughter ring through halls and cheer,
Toasting marshmallows with good friends near.
For in the glow where joys ignite,
We deck the halls with pure delight!

A Tapestry of Love and Wonder

Grandma's cookies, a sight to adore,
Each bite brings giggles, who could want more?
Sprinkles fall like confetti on the floor,
Chocolate chips and laughter we store.

A gift that squeaks hides under the tree,
A toy for the dog, oh what glee!
The reindeer parade makes us all cheer,
With Rudolph leading, we have no fear.

Snowball fights lead to laughter and shouts,
As mittens are lost, that's what it's about!
We'll wear mismatched socks, it's the latest trend,
With hot cocoa spills, let the fun never end!

Stories shared while we sip spiced brews,
With old family tales and comical views.
This gathering brings joy, wouldn't you say?
In the warmth of our hearts, it brightens the day!

Evergreen Hugs and Cinnamon Dreams

Trees in the living room, what a sight,
Needles drop everywhere, oh what fright!
As we sweep and giggle, with ornaments twirled,
Each sparkly bauble tells tales of the world.

Cinnamon candles flicker and tease,
While faux snow falls with matching ease.
The dog in a scarf prances around,
Creating a frenzy, chasing that sound.

Grandpa's jokes, they make us all moan,
Like reindeer in tights, awkward and prone.
With each punchline spilled, laughter breaks through,
As we gather 'round for a festive brew.

Gifts wrapped with care, and hardly a tear,
Unboxing surprises — is that a new deer?
In this chaos of joy, love seems to gleam,
With evergreen hugs and cinnamon dreams.

The Glow of Kindred Spirits

Candles flicker with joyful grace,
While Aunt Sue dances, a humorous pace.
She's getting down, arms flailing high,
While everyone laughs, too busy to cry.

Fruitcake's a mystery, who will take a slice?
Each bite's an adventure, oh isn't it nice?
With flavors galore, we can hardly resist,
Subject to laughter, it's hard to desist.

The stockings are hung with care, oh dear,
But Santa forgot, how could he be here?
With candy canes broken and puzzles unsolved,
Together we'll laugh, our worries dissolved.

So let's raise a glass to the memories we weave,
In this glow of bright spirits, our hearts we believe.
With each silly moment, we learn the sweet truth,
That joy's in the laughter, and always in youth!

Glints of Silver and Gold

A tree stands tall, all aglow,
With tinsel that sparkles, stealing the show.
Cats dive and leap, in a pouncing spree,
Chasing the glimmers, oh what a sight to see!

Hot cocoa spills, oh what a mess,
As marshmallows float, we can't help but confess.
The kids sneak cookies, with giggles galore,
While Santa's reindeer plot at the back door!

Gifts wrapped too tight, ribbons a maze,
Unraveling gifts, it's a tantalizing craze.
Each box is a treasure, a surprise in disguise,
Laughter erupts as chaos complies!

So here's to the season, with silly delight,
Where laughter and joy make everything bright.
In this whimsical world, we all play our part,
With glints of silver and gold in our heart!

A Cozy Nook of Delightful Moments

In a corner we gather, snug and secure,
With blankets and cocoa, of that we are sure.
A cat on the lap, snoring without care,
While we recount tales of holiday flair!

The fire crackles softly, a warm dance of light,
As grandpa starts snoring, what a comedic fright!
The dog chews a gift, it's a squeaky delight,
While Auntie debates if her sweater's too tight.

Cookies stack high, some gone in a flash,
Last year's holiday cards create quite the trash.
With jokes that are punny, we cackle and cheer,
In this cozy nook, all our troubles disappear!

So raise up a glass, to laughter and cheer,
To moments we cherish, year after year.
In this delightful corner, we join hand in hand,
In a tapestry woven, both funny and grand!

Expedition Through Frosted Nights

The snowflakes twirl in a wild ballet,
As we brave the cold in a clunky sleigh.
With mittens too big, we wobble and slide,
Chasing snowmen who seem to take pride!

Hot soup in a thermos, spills on my lap,
While someone declares, it's the ultimate map!
To hot cocoa stations, with toppings galore,
Oh, treasure awaits on this chilly outdoor tour!

A snowball launches, and chaos ensues,
Laughter erupts as we squabble and choose.
To build the best snowman, it's a race all around,
With carrots and scarves, our legends abound!

So onwards we journey, hearts filled with light,
Through frosted adventures, we laugh with delight.
In a world full of wonder, we dance and we play,
In this snowy escapade, come join us today!

The Dance of Shimmering Ornaments

Ornaments swinging on branches so low,
As we twist and twirl, creating our show.
Grandma's old favorites, a sight to be seen,
As we break into laughter through the evergreen!

The star on the top is starting to wobble,
As Uncle Joe dances, oh what a muddle!
With missteps and giggles, he throws us a spin,
While Aunt Betty wonders where she's been!

Each ornament tells a ridiculous tale,
Of the cat that got stuck in the wreath without fail.
We chuckle and cuddle on this jolly night,
As we share every story, it feels so right!

So raise your glass high, to memories made,
In a dance with the ornaments, let worries evade.
In this charming chaos, our laughter ignites,
A celebration of joy in these dazzling lights!

Snow Galaxies and Celebratory Harmonies

In the attic, toasts go clink,
I sip hot cocoa, can't help but blink.
Snowflakes dance with a silly jig,
Falling fast like a rabbit's twig.

Grandma's sweater, a sight to see,
Colors bright, like a fruit salad spree.
Elves on the shelf take moonlit leaps,
Laughing so hard, they spill their keeps!

We sing off-key but full of cheer,
Even the cat rolls its eyes in fear.
Lights on the house twinkle and sway,
As neighbors whisper, 'What a display!'

Snowmen wobble with carrot noses,
Wishing they had some better poses.
With winter games and laughter so bright,
We embrace the season, full of delight.

The Heartbeat of the Season

Bells are ringing, and so are we,
Dancing around like giddy bees.
Mistletoe hangs, but what a fright,
Who will kiss—oh, what a night!

Cookies burning, smoke fills the air,
Santa's sleigh stuck in a snow-filled glare.
The reindeer snicker, their eyes aglow,
As Rudolph! Pull that! Oh, how we'll blow!

Hot spiced cider, just one more round,
Who knew fun lived in holiday sound?
The star on top is a wobbly sight,
But with each giggle, everything feels right.

Jingle bells echo, the fun never ends,
A season where laughter and mischief bends.
Together we cherish, live each delightful day,
For in this heartbeat, joy leads the way.

An Ode to Cinnamon and Pine

Oh cinnamon, you spice of cheer,
In every cookie, you reappear.
Pine-scented dreams dance in the air,
A sniff, a shake, who needs to care?

The tree is lopsided, a brave, bold choice,
Yet we all cheer with a jubilant voice.
Needles drop, but who's keeping score?
It's decorated chaos, we all adore!

Wreaths on the door, just a bit wonky,
A family photo—oh, how funky!
Frosted windows hide laughter inside,
With jokes and puns, we take it in stride.

As carols blare, slippers do slide,
Everyone's laughing, let's take a ride!
With every bright moment that we trace,
Cinnamon and pine fill this merry space.

Flickering Flames of Shared Stories

In crackling fires, we share our tales,
Of great aunt Gertrude and her failed rails.
With laughter and gasps and an eye roll or two,
We weave silly stories shared by the crew.

Marshmallows roast, like clouds that we chase,
Sweet smiles mingle, each one finds its place.
Hot dogs fly with a sassy little spin,
Just when you thought where those chubby kiddos had been!

The night turns magical, but not without hitch,
Someone forgot the matches—oh, what a glitch!
Yet round campfire warmth, our hearts intertwine,
Finding joy together, like stars that brightly shine.

With each silly story, our bonds grow anew,
In flickering flames, laughter breaks through.
So here's to the moments we hold so dear,
In shared silly tales, the season is here!

The Gift of Silent Nights

In the quiet of the night, there's a sound,
A whisper from the fridge, oh what have you found?
Cookies left behind, with a wink and a grin,
Santa's belly rumbling, let the feast begin!

Reindeer hoofprints, oh what a chase,
One slipped on the roof, what a funny grace!
Shovels and snowballs, a battle in glee,
The frost on my nose makes me giggle with glee!

Gifts piled high, but socks still remain,
Granny claims her prize, oh it's all in vain!
Tinsel in my hair, like a festive crown,
I dance through the room, oh won't let me down!

So here's to the laughter, the cheer on display,
Let's toast to the moments that make our day!
With hot cocoa splashed, and a marshmallow sleigh,
Silent nights full of giggles, come what may!

Snowflakes and Mistletoe Dreams

Snowflakes are falling, oh what a sight,
But my nose is so cold, it can't start a fight!
Mistletoe hanging, but I dance with no care,
Who needs a kiss? Will just take a haircut here!

Elves on the shelf, they plot and they scheme,
One's stuck in the cookie jar, what a wild dream!
With giggles and laughter, we set them all free,
They promise to be nice, I'm still feeling queasy!

Pine needles stubbornly cling to my socks,
Try to sweep them away, but they just mock!
The cat's in the tree, it's a seasonal thrill,
While I sit on the couch, sipping cocoa, what a chill!

So here's to the chaos that makes moments bright,
With dreams of snowflakes, we dance through the night!
Mistletoe mischief, with laughter we beam,
What fun this December, oh what a grand dream!

Embracing the Glow of December

December has come, with lights all aglow,
But my hair's a disaster, in static it flows!
Jingle bells jingling, they dance down the street,
While I trip over twinkling, lost in my feet!

Hot chocolate spills, oh what a wild ride,
Marshmallows bounce around, with Santa to guide!
Wreaths so grand, I hang it too high,
Now it's swaying to music, oh my oh my!

Stockings are stuffed, with surprises galore,
But I found a toaster, never asked for more!
Singing out loud, out of tune but with glee,
The neighbors all laugh, as they peek out to see!

So let's embrace the madness, the glow of the day,
With laughter and fun, we'll dance and sway!
In a whirlwind of cheer, let our spirits soar,
December delights, who could ask for more?

Threads of Cheer and Brightness

Threads of cheer woven, in colors quite bold,
A scarf from Aunt Edna, oh if truth be told!
It tangled my head, like a festive crown,
Made me a walking yarn ball, I can't wear it down!

The tree's not too straight, it leans a bit shy,
It's auditioning for sitcoms, why even try?
Ornaments wobble, like dancers in line,
Bumping and crashing, what a sparkly time!

Gingerbread men hiding, oh where can they be?
One's taking a nap, another climbed a tree!
Frosting explosions, in flour I'm lost,
What fun for a baker, what a silly cost!

So here's to the threads, of fun and delight,
Stitching up laughter, through day and through night!
With bits of confusion, and joy intertwined,
In the quilt of this season, true magic we find!

A Tale of Nocturnal Glow

On a chilly night, with snowflakes fly,
Santa's rerouted, oh my, oh my!
Elves doing salsa by the bright firelight,
While reindeer giggle, what a silly sight!

Cookies left out, just a crumb or two,
Rudolph's munching, as the others do.
Milk's not for sipping, it's a reindeer splash,
Turns out they party, Oh! What a clash!

Jingle bells ringing, but not in tune,
Dancing with snowmen, one slips like a loon.
A penguin shivers, wearing a scarf too tight,
As laughter echoes through the frosty night.

So if you hear giggles up in the sky,
It's just merry chaos where the elves fly high!
With bells on their toes and joys in their hearts,
Spreading the cheer in their quirky arts!

Cradle of Seasonal Wishes

In a land where snow grows like cotton candy,
A squirrel with style goes a bit dandy.
He dons a hat, snazzy and bright,
As he drafts his wish list in the pale moonlight.

The gingerbread houses skimp on the glue,
Fell down once more! Oh, what to do?
A bunny in boots starts to chime,
"Last year's wishes? Hey, let's keep it prime!"

The carolers sing but, oh, what a tune,
While the cat gets scared of a little raccoon.
Shouted a snowflake, "I'm the star of the show!"
But it melted away, oh no, oh no!

So gather your giggles, let laughter flow,
In this cradle where whimsical wishes grow.
With fudge and laughter, we'll make it right,
Celebrating the joys of this grand winter night!

Woven Wishes Beneath the Tree

Beneath the tree with lights all aglow,
A kitten plays tag with a bow, oh no!
Tinsel gets tangled around little paws,
As they knock over gifts—what a merry cause!

The ornaments jingle as they try to hide,
Falling like stars on a festive ride.
A penguin attends with a wooly crown,
Conspiring to steal away the cookies down!

The stockings are drooping, all filled to the brim,
With candy canes hanging, what a bright whim!
But the dog thinks they're toys, and who can resist?
As he pounces in joy, "Wait, was that on the list?"

So gather round closely, let's share a cheer,
For laughter and joy make the best souvenir.
Woven wishes fly high, we toast and we sway,
Celebrating the madness in our own crazy way!

The Lullaby of Frost and Firelight

In sweaters too big, the family convenes,
With cocoa in hand and silly routines.
Grandpa's lost track of the names in the song,
But we all join in, and can't go wrong!

As snow twirls down like confetti of white,
The dog leaps and catches, what a funny sight!
Cats perched on mantles, judging us all,
While we tell silly tales of that one epic fall!

Muffins are burning—oops, dinner's a 'flop',
Santa's pets giggle, they just might pop!
The lights on the tree flicker and play,
As Frosty gets wobbly and sways away!

So here's to the moments wrapped in delight,
With laughter and warmth, call it a night.
We hum to the rhythm where joy takes its flight,
In our own little world of frost and firelight!

Starlit Skies and Family Ties

Under the twinkling, shimmering haze,
Uncles are dancing in silly displays.
Aunties are laughing, it tickles the night,
As cousins spin tales, oh what a sight!

Cookies are flying, and so are the pies,
Watch out for Grandma, she's quick on her spies!
Whispers of secrets and giggles abound,
These wacky traditions keep us all bound.

Pajamas in patterns, mismatch is key,
Mom's wearing slippers, as bright as can be.
Dad starts to snore, with eggnog in hand,
As the snowflakes outside decorate the land.

Silly hats on, we all strike a pose,
Frosty the snowman can't match how it glows.
Family together, like birds of a feather,
Oh, what a mingle! We're light as a feather!

Cherished Moments in the Ether

In the living room chaos, it's all out of whack,
Dad's trying to fix the lights on the pack.
Sisters are fighting who gets the last treat,
While dog's on the couch, with crumbs at his feet.

Grandpa's old stories, unable to quit,
Funny old rhymes that don't seem to fit.
Missed the punchline, but we all clap and cheer,
'Til someone spills cider, and begins the near.

Tinsel hangs low, like some fuzzy green beard,
Snowman outside looks slightly leered.
We giggle and chuckle at everything seen,
When popcorn is strung up, it's quite the machine!

Hats made of paper, yet we wear them with pride,
Grab all the presents and toss 'em inside!
Laughter it echoes, from hall into room,
Magic in moments, like kitchen's perfume.

Hearthside Tales and Flickering Flames

Sitting by fireside, our toes getting warm,
Dad tries to tell spooky tales with no charm.
We roll our eyes as he shares the last dread,
While marshmallows roast until they're all red.

Hot cocoa in mugs, topped with whipped cream,
Sips turn to giggles, it's all like a dream.
Mom starts her laughter, and soon we all laugh,
As clingy old tinsel falls off the giraffe.

The cat's on the mantle, and oh what a show,
He leaps for a ball, and the bulbs all aglow!
"You better not break them!" we all tend to shout,
But fair warning comes too late, oh no, what a rout!

Mom's baked a pie, with a crust like a maze,
It smells so good, we are all in a daze.
Together we mingle, like fruits in a stew,
With silly traditions, there's always one new!

Frostbitten Echoes of Nostalgia

Frost on the windows, and snow on the lawn,
Yet still we dance like the day we were born.
With mittens mismatched and hats that are threadbare,
We spin in the yard without any care.

The carols roll out from the mouth of the phone,
Yet Uncle Joe's voice reaches every stone.
Singing off-key, yet we don't seem to mind,
His jokes keep us laughing, no matter how blind.

Stories of Christmases from long ago,
Each recounting brings giggles, like tickles from snow.
Grandma once baked a cake, best you'd ever try,
But this year her secret was just a big lie!

Wrapping up memories with ribbons so bright,
Spilling hot chocolate, oh what a delight!
As we snuggle and chuckle in soft, cozy pajamas,
These silly traditions create laughter and drama!

Chiming Bells and Soft Footfalls

Jingle bells that bounce and sway,
Like kittens dancing in the fray.
Snowmen wobble, gifts in hand,
While reindeer plot a funny stand.

Tommy's hat flew off his head,
Chased by dogs, he'd rather dread!
Laughter echoes through the night,
As mischief blooms in pure delight.

Mittens lost upon the floor,
Who needs them when there's snow galore?
Cookies vanish, crumbs remain,
Santa's joy is our free gain.

Bells are ringing, gifts take flight,
Silly socks add to our plight.
In this fun and frosty cheer,
We'll toast marshmallows and good beer!

The Trail of Kindness and Grace

Sleight of hand with a cheeky grin,
A tangle of lights, that's how we begin.
Hot cocoa spills, coats go awry,
Laughing at the chaos, oh me, oh my!

Snowflakes dance with sheer delight,
While Grandma twirls in the moonlight.
Mom's lost her shoe, Dad's in a spin,
Let's make this a contest—who can win?

Elves in pajamas, oh what a sight!
Gift wraps flying in a colorful flight.
Happiness found in the mess we make,
Snowball fights are the memories we take.

With kindness wrapped, we spread the cheer,
Even if the cat's been steered clear.
Laughter loops around each grace,
Together we giggle in this wonderful place!

A Canvas of Seasonal Splendor

Glistening lights in a beautiful row,
Neighbors peeking through the trees aglow.
Reindeer prancing in sequined suits,
While gingerbread folks adorn our boots.

Painter's brush drips with bright hues,
Catch the cat sneaking sips of our brews!
Ornaments precariously hung,
One more tumble, we'll have a fun song sung!

Snowflakes whisper, the fireplace crackles,
Grandpa's snoring—oh, the funny cackles!
With giggles mixed in with holiday cheer,
We paint memories that bring us near.

An easel of laughter, a palette of grace,
In this festive carnival space.
Creativity flows, we'll never tire,
Building joy and dreams—our hearts catch fire!

Tides of Hope and Togetherness

Surfing through the waves of cheer,
Tangled lights make the spirits clear.
Laughter booms, it's a bumpy ride,
As grandma's old sweater makes the slide.

Elves on roller skates take a chance,
Crashing into the Christmas dance.
They giggle and wiggle with zany style,
While kids join in, grinning all the while.

Eggnog spills in a modern art way,
Creating smiles, what can we say?
We gather 'round with plates piled high,
Sharing stories while sparks fly.

As seasons shift in a merry swirl,
Holding hands, we give a twirl.
Together we laugh, together we play,
In the glow of the festive holiday!

Jubilant Spirits in a Winter Wonderland

In a hat that's far too big, they prance,
The snowmen dance, oh what a chance!
With carrots for noses and smiles so bright,
They twirl and spin in pure delight.

The sleds fly down the hills with glee,
With snowballs whizzing, oh dear me!
A snowball fight, who'll take the blame?
We're all in stitches, it's quite the game!

Hot cocoa's brewing, marshmallows afloat,
Laughter and giggles, we're all in the boat.
Mom's cookie stash is running low,
Whose turn is it now? Oh, where did they go?

Jubilant spirits chase away the gloom,
As snowflakes dance, they fill every room.
With jingle bells ringing and faces aglow,
The fun ends not, oh no, no, no!

The Starlit Promise of Tomorrow

Under twinkling stars, we make a pact,
A wish on a star, a little abstract.
But while we stare up at the magical light,
Someone trips over a gift—oh, what a sight!

With reindeer antics and Santa's big laugh,
We plot secret plans for a sly little half.
'Oh shame on you!', a child cries in glee,
While cats chase ribbons up near the tree.

The promise of tomorrow—cookies galore,
Who'll find the last one? A fierce tug-of-war!
While socks filled with candy dangle so high,
We sneak in the treats, oh my, oh my!

Each moment is silly, each joke so bright,
In the glow of the stars, everything's right.
A dance in the snow, a slip and a fall,
The night's full of laughter; we cherish it all.

Resting in the Glow of Togetherness

Gathered around with loved ones so dear,
As stories unfold, we all lend an ear.
The cat finds a spot, nestles in tight,
Nothing quite beats this cozy delight.

Grandpa starts snoring, a soft little buzz,
While we giggle and tease him—oh, what a fuss!
The game of charades begins with big flair,
As we act out a turkey, none seem to care.

The glow of the fire warms hearts and our toes,
With cookies still baking, oh how time goes!
We sing off-key, forming our own song,
In this glow of togetherness, we all belong.

So let's raise a glass filled with cheer and good will,
To moments like these that always fulfill.
With laughter and love, the night carries on,
In the warmth of our joy, we find where we've shone.

Festive Echoes of the Heart

The echoes of laughter fill every space,
As we bumble through kitchens, a comical race.
With flour on faces and gifts in a pile,
We wrap up the giggles; we wrap with a smile.

'Tis the season for chaos—who burned the cake?
A holiday mishap, a big frosted flake.
Yet with merry hearts, we gather around,
For festive echoes of joy can be found.

Elf hats on heads, mismatched in design,
Trying to juggle, we giggle and whine.
Each ornament hung with a dotted mistake,
Yet it's perfect, for we've got what it takes.

As carols ring out and the lights flicker bright,
We dance through the evening, all heart and goodnight.
In laughter we find joy, in chaos a spark,
This festive season sings loud in the dark.

Luminescent Pathways Through the Snow

Twinkling lights dance with glee,
While snowflakes play hide and seek.
A squirrel stole my scarf, oh no!
He wears it proudly, what a show!

Footprints lead to mischief's door,
Where eggnog glows, and giggles soar.
The dog dives deep in cotton white,
Sniffing out treats, what a delight!

Snowmen wobble, hats askew,
Juggling carrots, who knew?
A snowball flies, oh my, oh dear!
Did that just take out my holiday cheer?

With laughter bound in frosty air,
The moon grins wide, a snowy fair.
We're all just kids beneath this glow,
In a wonderland of fluff and woe.

A Festival of Heartfelt Togetherness

Gather 'round the feast so bright,
With grandma's cookies, pure delight.
Uncle Fred tells jokes, a loud guffaw,
We laugh until we nearly fall!

The cat plays with the ribboned bows,
While grandpa snores, oh how it shows!
Mismatched socks on everyone's feet,
It's the fashion of love, oh so sweet!

The punch is spiked, or is it just me?
Snowballs inside, a cheeky spree.
A dance-off starts right by the tree,
With moves so wild, none can foresee!

We sing off-key, with voices bold,
Tales of holiday mishaps retold.
Together we shine, so warm, so bright,
What a lovely, goofy, festive night!

Gentle Boughs and Holiday Whispers

The pine tree's dressed in shimmering flair,
But the cat's up there without a care!
Baubles fall like a clumsy gale,
And ornaments dance a jingling tale.

The elf on the shelf, with a smirk so sly,
Hides every day, like he can fly.
We search high and low, what a fun game!
Found him in the kitchen, stirring with fame!

A wreath hung crooked, but who can fuss?
It adds to the charm, just like all of us.
Joy spills from mugs, hot cocoa delight,
As we share our secrets deep into the night.

Gifts wrapped in laughter, some slightly torn,
With tape that was borrowed, now forlorn.
The spirit flows, in cozy homes,
Through gentle boughs, where humor roams.

Magic Markers on the Calendar

December glows with colors bright,
Each day a party, pure delight.
Mark the dates with scribbles and cheer,
For every whimsy that draws us near!

An advent calendar's such a tease,
Behind the doors, what do we seize?
Chocolate, trinkets, or a pair of socks,
Each day reveals a fun paradox.

The countdown brings wonders, oh what a thrill,
With each passing hour, there's more to fulfill.
Grandma's karaoke, not so divine,
Yet we cheer and dance, out of line!

So pass the pen, let's scribble some joy,
With plans to mischief, let's outsmart the boy!
Magic awaits in each little note,
This season of fun, a joyful antidote.

Mirth and Merriment Wrapped in Light

On rooftops high, the reindeer prance,
While Uncle Fred attempts a dance.
He slips on ice, oh what a sight,
Our laughter echoes through the night.

The cookies vanish, crumbs abound,
As cats plot mischief all around.
The lights all twinkle, and the cat's awake,
Chasing shadows, for goodness' sake!

Grandma's sweater, knit with flair,
Looks like a gift from a bear's lair.
We smile and tease, it's all in fun,
A family roast has just begun!

Mirthful moments, sweet and bright,
Filled with joy and pure delight.
Together we dance, all aglow,
In this funny, festive show!

A Symphony of Festive Wishes

In the kitchen, pots collide,
While turkey legs take a slide.
The dog barks loud, it joins the fun,
Trying to steal a baked sweet bun.

The carols play, a humorous tune,
As Dad makes up words to everyone's swoon.
With every note, a giggle escapes,
As we all join in, making shapes.

Nutcrackers dance on the window sill,
While naughty elves plot their next thrill.
A mix-up with gifts causes a stir,
"Who got my socks?" becomes a blur!

Through giggles and smiles, we find our way,
In this symphony of joyous play.
Around the tree, we all can see,
Together forever, just you and me!

Tinsel Dreams and Snowy Dawns

The snowflakes fall, a magical sight,
But Johnny's snowman's just not right.
With a carrot nose that's quite absurd,
It looks like it's joined the circus herd!

Tinsel tangled on the floor,
Mom's exasperation, we just adore.
With wrapping paper flying wide,
Gift unwrapping's a wild ride!

Schroeder's piano, a playful mess,
Each note played like a mini chess.
As we all join in with a cringe,
This symphony has quite the binge!

We laugh, and joke, with joy in view,
Tinsel dreams painted just for you.
Through funny quirks, our spirits soar,
In this winter's grand folklore!

The Glow of Hopes Reborn

The fireplace crackles, a warm embrace,
But watch out closely, that dancing lace!
It's Grandma's scarf around the flame,
Her knitting skills will face some blame!

The stockings hang, a curious sight,
Filled with treasures, what a delight!
An orange, some socks, and a toy that grins,
We laugh and ponder what good fortune wins!

With fudge that's stuck to the ceiling high,
We marvel at how the seasons fly.
Just sticky fingers and merry cheer,
Each scrumptious bite brings everyone near.

Hope and laughter float in the air,
With chilly winds and festive flair.
We dance and sing, a joyous cue,
In this moment, all dreams come true!